Glaciers

by Lisa Trumbauer

Table of Contents

Introduction

Glaciers cover one-tenth of Earth's surface. Most of Earth's fresh water is frozen in glaciers.

Glaciers move very slowly. Glaciers change Earth very slowly.

What are glaciers? How do glaciers form? How do glaciers change Earth? Read to learn about glaciers.

▲ These people can see a glacier.

Words to Know

cirques

fiords

glaciers

icebergs

ice sheets

moraines

piedmont glaciers

valley glaciers

See the Glossary on page 30.

What Are Glaciers?

Glaciers are large areas of ice and snow. The ice and snow move very slowly.

Some glaciers are in mountains. Some glaciers hang on mountains. Some glaciers are in **cirques**.

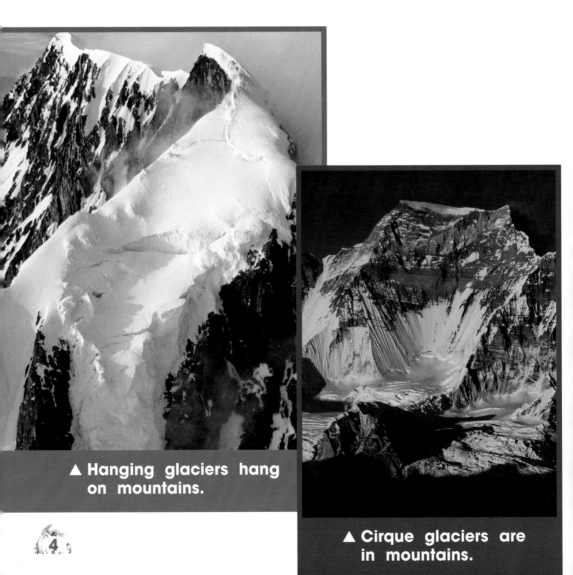

▲ Hanging glaciers hang on mountains.

▲ Cirque glaciers are in mountains.

Some glaciers are in mountain valleys. These glaciers look like rivers of ice and snow.

Valley glaciers move down mountains. Rocks and dirt break off Earth. The rocks and dirt are in the glaciers.

▲ Valley glaciers have pieces of rock and dirt.

Valley glaciers move down mountains. Some valley glaciers move onto flat plains. The glaciers move over the land. These glaciers are **piedmont glaciers**.

IT'S A FACT

The Malaspina Glacier is about the size of Rhode Island.

▲ **This glacier is a piedmont glacier. This glacier is Malaspina Glacier. It is in Alaska.**

Some glaciers are huge pieces of ice. The pieces of ice are **ice sheets**.

A huge ice sheet covers Antarctica. Another ice sheet covers most of Greenland.

Did You Know?

Antarctica is a continent.

▲ **The Antarctic ice sheet is very large.**

Scientists think the ice sheets are very old. Ice covered much of Earth long ago.

Then, Earth got warmer. Much of the ice melted. Antarctica and Greenland did not get warmer. The ice did not melt.

Solve This

The Antarctic ice sheet is more than one mile thick. The ice sheet is more than how many feet thick?

Answer: 5,280 feet

▲ The ice in Antarctica and Greenland did not melt.

Sometimes glaciers are near an ocean or sea. Pieces of the glaciers break off. The pieces fall into the water. The pieces in the water are **icebergs**.

▲ Icebergs are pieces of glaciers.

Did You Know?

- *Berg* is the German word for "mountain."
- Most of an iceberg is under the water.
- Icebergs have pieces of rock and soil. The rock and soil get into the water.
- The *Titanic* was a ship. The *Titanic* hit an iceberg. The *Titanic* sank.

How Do Glaciers Form?

Glaciers form in places that have cold winters. The places have cool summers.

Snow falls in the cold places. Some of the snow melts. Then, the melted snow freezes. The melted snow is ice.

▲ Many mountains are cold in the winter. The mountains are cool in the summer. Glaciers can form in these mountains.

More snow falls on the ice. This snow melts and freezes. More ice is made. The new ice packs down the old ice. The ice is very heavy. The snow and ice make a glacier.

Try This

The bottom of a glacier is packed down ice. The bottom of a glacier does not have air bubbles.

Look at an ice cube. Does the ice cube have air bubbles? Is the ice packed down?

A glacier can change size. A glacier can get larger with more snow.

▲ This is the Riggs Glacier in 1979.

Sometimes there is not much snow. The temperature gets warmer. Some of the glacier melts. The glacier gets smaller.

▲ This is the Riggs Glacier in 1993. Some of the glacier melted.

The Antarctic ice sheet does not change much. Antarctica does not get much snow. The ice sheet does not grow much.

IT'S A FACT

Antarctica is a desert. It is a desert because it gets so little rain or snow.

Antarctica is very cold. The ice does not melt much. The ice sheet does not get much smaller.

▲ The ice sheet in Antarctica does not change much.

Chapter 3

How Do Glaciers Change Earth?

Most glaciers move very slowly. Mountain glaciers move down mountains. The rocks and dirt move with the glaciers.

The glaciers form valleys as they move. The glaciers pick up pieces of rocks and dirt. The glaciers move the rocks and dirt. The rocks and dirt move away from the mountains.

Did You Know?

Some glaciers move a few feet every year. Some glaciers move a few feet every day.

▲ A glacier formed this valley. The valley is in Italy.

Glaciers can make valleys near an ocean or sea. The valleys fill with water. Then, the valleys are **fiords**.

▲ A glacier formed this fiord. The fiord is in Norway.

Glaciers can push up rock and dirt. Glaciers can push the rock and dirt into hills. These hills are **moraines**.

▲ A glacier formed this moraine. The moraine is in Nevada.

21

Sometimes glaciers make huge holes. The holes fill with water. Then, the holes are lakes.

▲ A glacier formed this lake. The lake is in the Himalaya Mountains.

Glaciers can make cirques. Glaciers rub away part of a mountain.

▲ **A glacier formed this cirque. The cirque is in Montana.**

Glaciers can change the shape of mountains. Some mountains are shaped like horns.

▲ **A glacier formed this mountain. The mountain is the Matterhorn. It is in Switzerland.**

Glaciers can break huge pieces from mountains. The shapes of the mountains change. Then, the mountains have steep cliffs.

▲ **A glacier broke pieces from this mountain. The mountain is Half Dome. It is in California.**

25

Glaciers changed Earth in many places. Maybe a glacier formed a lake where you swim. Maybe a glacier formed a mountain where you climb. Maybe a glacier formed a valley where you live.

▲ Glaciers formed lakes.

Glaciers move very slowly. Glaciers change Earth very slowly.

Did You Know?

Glacier ice is very old. Some glacier ice has frozen plants and animals. The plants and animals are very old. Scientists study the old plants and animals.

Summary

Glaciers are large areas of ice and snow. There are many different types of glaciers. Glaciers change the shape of Earth in many ways.

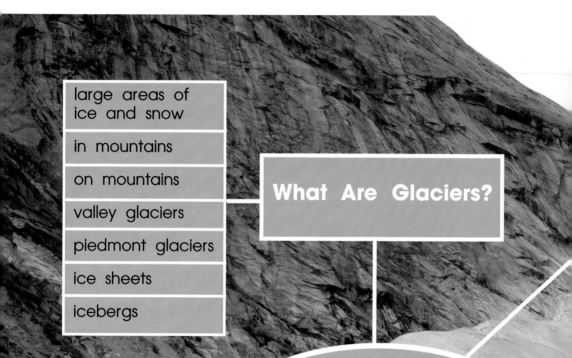

large areas of ice and snow

in mountains

on mountains

valley glaciers

piedmont glaciers

ice sheets

icebergs

What Are Glaciers?

Glaciers

Think About It

1. How do glaciers form?
2. How do icebergs form?
3. How do glaciers change mountains?

How Do Glaciers Form?

Snow melts and then freezes.

More snow melts and then freezes.

New ice packs down old ice.

Some glaciers form in mountains.

Some glaciers change size.

How Do Glaciers Change Earth?

move rocks and dirt

form valleys

form moraines

form lakes

form cirques

shape mountains

form cliffs

Glossary

cirques areas in mountains rubbed away by glaciers

*Glaciers can be in **cirques**.*

fiords valleys made by glaciers; the valleys fill with water

*Norway has many **fiords**.*

glaciers large areas of ice and snow

Glaciers change Earth.

icebergs pieces of glaciers in the water

Icebergs have pieces of rocks and soil.

ice sheets huge pieces of ice

Ice sheets cover Antarctica and Greenland.

moraines rock and dirt hills

Glaciers make moraines.

piedmont glaciers glaciers that come down mountains onto plains

The Malaspina Glacier is a piedmont glacier.

valley glaciers glaciers in valleys

Valley glaciers look like rivers of ice and snow.

31

Index